SHOCK ZONE
DEADLY AND DANGEROUS

DEADLY
Danger
ZONES

SANDY DONOVAN

Lerner Publications Company • Minneapolis

Lerner Publications Company
A division of Lerner Publishing Group, Inc.
241 First Avenue North
Minneapolis, MN 55401 U.S.A.

Website address: www.lernerbooks.com

Library of Congress Cataloging-in-Publication Data

Donovan, Sandra, 1967–
    Deadly Danger Zones / by Sandy Donovan.
        p.   cm. — (Shockzone™—deadly and dangerous)
    Includes index.
    ISBN 978–1–4677–0600–1 (lib. bdg. : alk. paper)
    1.Voyages and travels—Juvenile literature. 2.Wilderness survival—
Juvenile literature. I. Title.
G570.D66 2013
910.4—dc23   2012018237

Manufactured in the United States of America
1 – BP – 12/31/12

TABLE OF CONTENTS

PACK YOUR BAGS! OR DON'T

Wondering where to find the world's **most dangerous spots?** We're talking the homes of man-eating tigers and hungry crocodiles. We're talking places with deadly plants, poisonous gases, and a fire that has burned for years.

DANGER

Turn the page to discover a place where swimmers become shark snacks.

Maybe you'd like to visit one of these places. Or maybe you just want to know where to stay away from! Either way, this book will give you all the gory details you need. But be careful. You might uncover some dangers you didn't even know existed!

NEW SOUTH WALES, AUSTRALIA

Of all the ways to die, having a great white shark gnaw your limbs off would be one of the worst. Do you agree? Then you might want to stay away from New South Wales, Australia. This area has the highest number of shark-attack deaths in the world.

Most great whites are between 13 and 16 feet (4 to 5 meters) long. They can weigh up to 4,200 pounds (1,900 kilograms). Their expert hearing and smelling help them spot prey easily. Their double rows of sawlike teeth let them tear off huge chunks of flesh. But lucky us, great whites don't really like to eat humans. Why? Too bony. Most

Researchers say more than 170 shark-on-human attacks have hit New South Wales in the last two centuries. Of those attacks, 55 ended in death. So what is it about this area? Are the sharks extra hungry? Are the people extra tasty?

Scientists have another idea. They think it may be the narrow continental shelf along these shores. In plain English: deep water is closer to the shore in New South Wales than in other places. Swimmers tend to stay close to shore. And sharks tend to live in deep water. What happens when the shore gets as close to deep water as it does in New South Wales? You guessed it! A buffet for great whites.

continental shelf = the stretch of shallow water found around the edge of each continent. At the edge of this shelf, the ground drops off sharply.

SAFER WATERS?

Think you're safer staying close to home? Think again. The U.S. Pacific coast is the shark attack capital of the world. People there have reported more than 150 shark attacks over the years!

7

MOUNT VESUVIUS

Maybe you've heard the story of Pompeii. The Italian city was buried in lava in A.D. 79. A volcano erupted at nearby Mount Vesuvius. Historians think at least two thousand people died. Lava wiped out some people. Ash buried others. But the heat of the explosion killed most victims.

You may be thinking, "So what?" That was nearly two thousand years ago. The danger's over. Well, not quite.

Once a volcano erupts, there's always a chance it will erupt again. Mount Vesuvius has erupted more than thirty times since it buried Pompeii. An eruption in 1906 killed one hundred people. These days, about three million people live near Mount Vesuvius. Most of them live in the city of Naples. More people live within 100

The volcano known as Mount Vesuvius overlooks the city of Naples.

miles (161 kilometers) of Vesuvius than near any other volcano in the world. The volcano hasn't erupted since 1944. But there's no reason to think it's going to stay mellow forever.

Would you take the chance and live near this danger zone? Here's something to think about while you decide. Scientists have said the next eruption will move fast. That means there could be no time to get out before the lava pours down.

This person couldn't escape Pompeii before the eruption of A.D. 79. Hardened lava has preserved the person's body for nearly two thousand years.

Miyakejima Island, Japan

What could be scarier than an erupting volcano? How about a volcano that spits out poisonous gas? A volcano sits atop the tiny island of Miyakejima in Japan. It's called Mount Oyama. This volcano has erupted several times in the last hundred years. In 2000 people left the island after an eruption. After that, Mount Oyama continued to send harmful sulfur gas into the air. This made the air unhealthful to breathe. People were banned from the island for more than four years.

Later, about twenty-five hundred people returned to Miyakejima. There's still a lot of sulfur in the air. Everyone on the island carries a gas mask at all times. Seriously—it's a law. You don't have to

The people of Miyakejima wear gas masks as part of daily life.

wear the mask. But you have to have it ready. The government tracks the air quality. If they notice too much sulfur in the air, they sound an alarm. Everyone straps on a mask.

Think that sounds like a crazy vacation spot? Some people think it sounds great. The island is popular with tourists. You can take a boat there from Japan's mainland. And don't worry. As soon as you step onshore, you can pick up a gas mask at one of many stores.

COUGH! SULFUR GAS!

When a volcano erupts, it spews out sulfur gas. This poisonous gas is also known as sulfur dioxide. It can be deadly to people and animals who breathe too much of it. Even breathing a little can cause illness and possibly death.

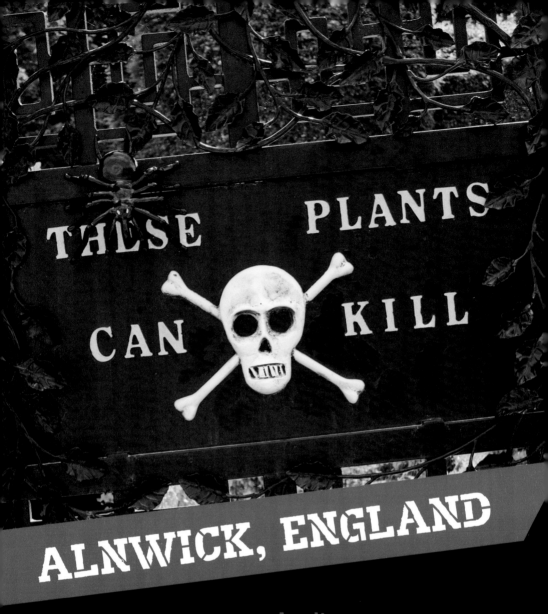

THESE PLANTS CAN KILL

ALNWICK, ENGLAND

If you end up in this danger spot, don't say you weren't warned. To enter the Alnwick Poison Garden, you have to pass through a gate marked with a skull and crossbones. To make sure visitors get the point, the gate also carries the warning "THESE PLANTS CAN KILL." This garden in England contains nearly one hundred types of poisonous plants. Some can kill you instantly. Others will poison you just enough to make you wish you were dead.

The deadliest plants are kept behind cages. But stay on the safe side. Keep your hands to yourself as you tour the grounds.

These orange berries look tasty, but they will make your tongue tingle—a sign that the poison is working.

Who in their right mind would start a garden of deadly plants? In this case, it was the Duchess of Northumberland. She's just an average plant-loving member of the British aristocracy. In 2001 the Duchess opened the Alnwick Garden on her estate in Alnwick, England. This garden shows off rare plants from around the world. It became a hot spot for tourists. A few years later, the Duchess added the Alnwick Poison Garden. Luckily for visitors, she keeps the poisonous plants in their own gated area!

aristocracy = people of noble families

A NOBLE HISTORY

The Duchess of Northumberland wasn't the first aristocrat to dream up a deadly garden. In the late Middle Ages (about 1200 to 1500), the Medici family ruled northern Italy. They kept gardens of deadly plants. But there's one difference between these gardens and the Alnwick Poison Garden. Enemies of the Medici family often turned up dead from poisoning. The Duchess is happy just to show visitors rare plants!

Catherine de Medici

The Sunderbans

The Sunderbans is a forest in Asia. It's partly in India and partly in Bangladesh. This area is home to many natural disasters. Tropical storms have struck the area. So have floods and mudslides. But the Sunderbans is deadly even when the weather's nice. The danger comes from tigers.

About six hundred Bengal tigers live in the Sunderbans. In fact, the forest is the largest home to tigers in the world. This alone shouldn't make the area dangerous. Humans aren't a tiger's favorite food. Most tigers won't even attack a person if they come across one napping in a forest! But Bengal tigers in the Sunderbans really like to eat people. They ate about fifty people each year during the twentieth century. In recent times, that number has dropped to just a few each year.

What makes tigers attack humans? Scientists have a few ideas about why tigers in the Sunderbans have attacked so many humans. People have hunted tigers heavily in other parts of the world. They have not hunted tigers as heavily in the Sunderbans. Other tigers may have learned to fear humans after being hunted. But the Sunderbans tigers never learned that lesson.

The area's weather may also have to do with the attacks. Many locals have died from natural disasters. Their bodies have floated in rivers through the Sunderbans. Tigers may have gotten used to eating humans in this way. Perhaps those dead humans were so tasty that the tigers decided they wanted more.

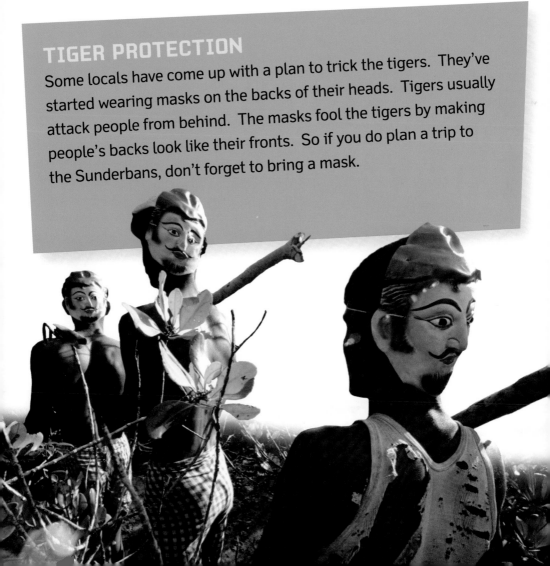

TIGER PROTECTION

Some locals have come up with a plan to trick the tigers. They've started wearing masks on the backs of their heads. Tigers usually attack people from behind. The masks fool the tigers by making people's backs look like their fronts. So if you do plan a trip to the Sunderbans, don't forget to bring a mask.

QUEIMADA GRANDE, BRAZIL

No one lives on the island of Queimada Grande. Why not? Here's a clue. The place's nickname is Snake Island. This small island off the coast of Brazil is chock-full of snakes. Scientists say there are between one and five snakes for every 10.8 square feet (1 sq. meter). The island is about 0.2 square miles (430,000 sq. m) large. We'll do the math. That means between 430,000 and 2.15 million snakes are crawling around this one small island.

These aren't just any snakes, either. These are golden lanceheads. They're one of the most venomous snakes in the world. Golden lanceheads have caused more than 90 percent of all snakebite deaths in Brazil.

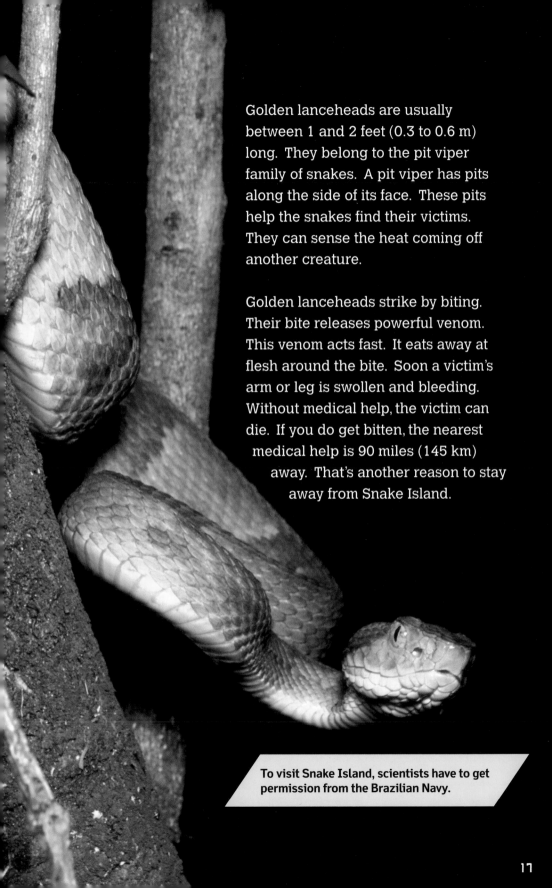

Golden lanceheads are usually between 1 and 2 feet (0.3 to 0.6 m) long. They belong to the pit viper family of snakes. A pit viper has pits along the side of its face. These pits help the snakes find their victims. They can sense the heat coming off another creature.

Golden lanceheads strike by biting. Their bite releases powerful venom. This venom acts fast. It eats away at flesh around the bite. Soon a victim's arm or leg is swollen and bleeding. Without medical help, the victim can die. If you do get bitten, the nearest medical help is 90 miles (145 km) away. That's another reason to stay away from Snake Island.

To visit Snake Island, scientists have to get permission from the Brazilian Navy.

DERWEZE, TURKMENISTAN

A burning hole blazes in the central Asian village of Derweze. It's 230 feet (70 m) wide and really, really hot. Locals call this ring of fire the Gate to the Underworld. Well, sometimes they use a different word for "underworld." But you get the drift.

underworld = in myth, a gloomy place where people go after they die

How did this oversized fire pit end up in the middle of a desert? Scientists put it there. But not on purpose. Here's the story.

In 1971 a group of scientists was exploring the area. They began drilling through the desert floor. The scientists made an amazing discovery. They found a huge cavern filled with harmful gas.

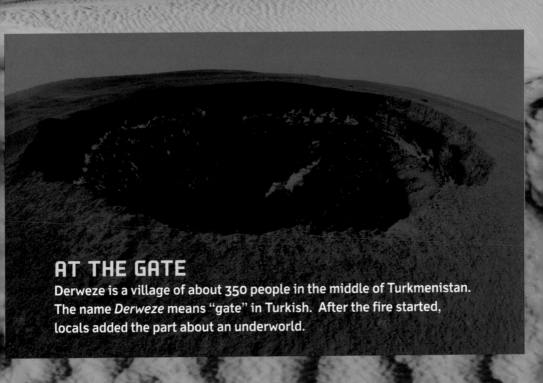

Derweze is in the middle of central Asia's Karakum Desert.

Soon the group's drill collapsed through the ground. The cavern became a gaping hole. *Hmm,* the scientists thought. *We'd better not let this gas leak all over the desert.* So they set fire to the gas. They figured it wouldn't take long to burn the gas away. They guessed maybe a few hours or a few days, at most. Quick thinking. But their guess was a little off. Forty years later, the hole is still burning.

AT THE GATE

Derweze is a village of about 350 people in the middle of Turkmenistan. The name *Derweze* means "gate" in Turkish. After the fire started, locals added the part about an underworld.

Ramree Island, Burma

If you like relaxing vacations, then stay away from Ramree Island in Burma (also called Myanmar). Sure, it's warm and sunny. And it has nice beaches. Well, it has so-so beaches. The land's more swampy than sandy. But that's not what's going to spoil your vacation. That job belongs to the island's wildlife.

Scorpions creep around Ramree Island. Mosquitoes buzz through the air. And a gang of crocodiles patrols the swampland. We're not just talking ordinary, everyday crocodiles either. We're talking saltwater crocs, the world's largest reptiles.

About one thousand saltwater crocs live on this tiny island. People discovered just how dangerous these crocs were during World War II (1939–1945). In January 1945, British and Japanese forces fought in the Battle of Ramree Island. The British backed four hundred or so Japanese soldiers into the swamps of Ramree. And living in those swamps were none other than the island's crocs. Not very many Japanese soldiers made it out of the swamps. The story goes that only about twenty soldiers were found alive.

British troops make their way to Ramree Island in 1945.

TRUE OR FALSE?

Some people don't believe the report of the Battle of Ramree Island. They think the report overstates the number of deaths. Maybe you think so too. If so, visit Ramree Island at your own risk! Really. We'll see you when (or *if*) you make it home ...

A crocodile of Ramree Island gets some sun.

THE YUNGAS ROAD, BOLIVIA

Few locals will drive across Bolivia's North Yungas Road without stopping to pray. They call this path the Road of Death.

What makes the road so risky? It cuts through a steep mountain. The Road of Death runs about 40 miles (64 km) between the cities of La Paz and Coroico. For most of the way, the road is less than 10 feet (3 m) wide. That's about as wide as most one-way streets. But the Yungas Road is a two-way road. Drivers have to figure out how to pass one another with just inches between them.

Drivers also have to make sure their wheels don't slide off the narrow road. The road's edge disappears into a drop-off that can be as high as 2,000 feet (610 m). Until recently no guardrails stood along the road either. If one wheel ran off the edge, the car or the

A group of bikers seeks a thrill along the Road of Death.

Before 2006 around three hundred people died on the North Yungas Road each year. That year a safer Yungas Road opened. This road is wider and less winding. It has guardrails too. Since 2006 fewer accidents have happened. Most drivers who aren't crazy decide to take the new road instead of the older one. But the old North Yungas Road is still a hit with downhill bike racers. So far, about twenty bikers have died after speeding off the cliff.

DALLOL, ETHIOPIA

Before you pack for a trip to Dallol in central Africa, you might want to root through your luggage. You won't be needing any sweaters, hats, or jackets. This rugged area in northern Ethiopia has a yearly average temperature of 94°F (34°C). It's so hot, about the only thing you'll need is water, water, and more water.

Dallol is basically a desert. Glowing yellow lava bubbles beneath the ground. Sometimes it seeps up through cracks too. The lava is left over from a volcano eruption in 1924. And oh yeah: earthquakes hit the area more often than most other places

A group of central Africa's Afar people draws water from a well.

Sounds like a tough place to live, right? But Africa's Afar people have called this spot home for hundreds of years. How do they do it? For one thing, they move often. The nomadic group sets up camp for a few months at a time. The men spend their days mining salt from thick white crusts that spread out over the desert. Then they form the salt into bricks and trade it for clothes and other items. Meanwhile, the women spend their days gathering water for the tribe. Once the Afar people have used up all of a spot's water, they move to a new home.

nomadic = a way of life where people move often in search of water, food, or land to farm

The Afar people use camels and donkeys to move salt blocks.

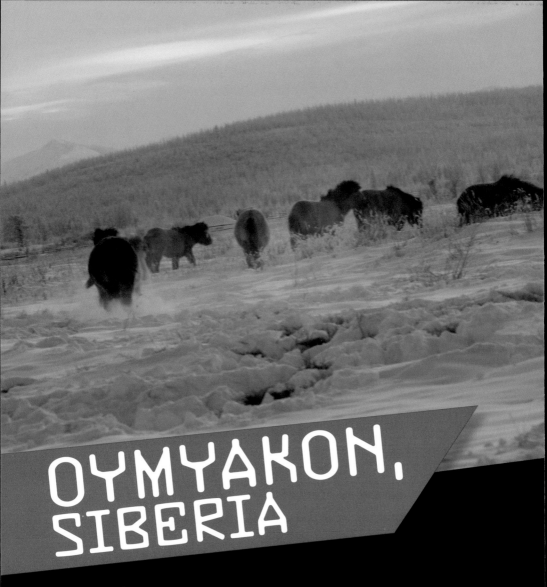

OYMYAKON, SIBERIA

Before going outside in Oymyakon, Russia, remember a few things. First, take off your sunglasses. If you don't, the cold weather might crack the lenses. Also, cover up as much of your body as possible. This will help you avoid instant frostbite, frozen eyelashes, and other effects of the cold. And if you arrive by car, make sure the driver parks indoors. Otherwise, the gas will freeze inside the gas tank.

Just how cold does it get in this tiny town in northern Russia? The average low temperature for January is –57°F (–50°C). But that's nothing compared to the record low. In 1924 a scientist recorded a temperature of –96.2°F (–71.2°C).

Siberia is the chilliest part of Russia. In the Siberian town of Oymyakon, hot water can freeze almost instantly.

Think you'd have to be nuts to live here? About five hundred people disagree. That's about the year-round population of Oymyakon. The townspeople have one store. But if you're looking to buy anything except bread, milk, or reindeer meat, you're probably out of luck. Still, life in Oymyakon can be fun. When kids want to have a snowball fight, all they have to do is toss a cup of boiling water into the air. It'll instantly turn to snow!

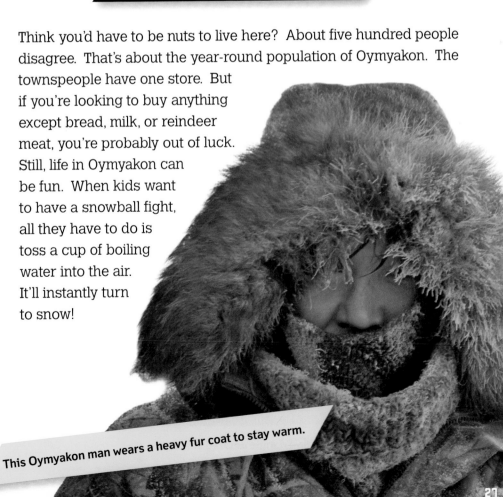

This Oymyakon man wears a heavy fur coat to stay warm.

THE BERMUDA TRIANGLE

The Bermuda Triangle is a stretch of the Atlantic Ocean with **a very bad rep.** This area is home to a number of unexplained ship, boat, and plane disappearances. Or is it?

The triangle reaches from the Bermudas to Puerto Rico to Florida. It covers several hundred thousand square miles. In the 1950s, people began to write about mysterious activities in the area. A newspaper article and then a magazine story described large numbers of ships or planes that entered the triangle...and never came out.

JUNE

AMAZING STORIES

Scientifiction Stories by
A. Hyatt Verrill
John W. Campbell, Jr.
Edmond Hamilton

Tales of the Bermuda Triangle amazed science fiction readers.

Was it bad luck? Paranormal activity? Soon books, TV shows, and films told of strange events within the Bermuda Triangle. A U.S. Navy plane, a large tanker ship, and a yacht had all disappeared on the water.

Is it really true that disappearances in the triangle are extra common? Most experts say no. They agree that a large number of planes, ships, and boats have gone missing there. But many of the disappearances can be explained by bad weather. Other claims have turned out to be completely false. The famous tanker ship actually disappeared in the Pacific Ocean, not the Atlantic.

paranormal = something unexplained by scientific facts

The bottom line: the Bermuda Triangle can be nasty during storms. But there's nothing paranormal about it.

FURTHER INFORMATION

Brazilian Snakes Project
http://www.brazilian-snakes.com/brazilian-snakes-resume.html
Do you find deadly snakes fascinating? Check out this book to learn more about golden lanceheads and how Brazil is trying to keep people safe from snakebites.

Cyber School Bus—United Nations
http://www.un.org/Pubs/CyberSchoolBus/index.shtml
Visit this site from the United Nations to learn about natural disasters, nuclear weapons, and other deadly threats from around the world.

Donovan, Sandy. *Lethal Leaders and Military Madmen.* Minneapolis: Lerner Publications, 2013. You've read up on danger zones. Next, brush up on history with a look at the world's cruelest conquerors.

My Wonderful World—National Geographic
http://www.mywonderfulworld.org/kidsteens_welcome.html
Learn more about destinations around the world, test your global IQ, and play games on the National Geographic site just for tweens and teens.

Orndorff, John C., and Suzanne Harper. *Terrorists, Tornadoes, and Tsunamis: How to Prepare for Life's Danger Zones.* New York: Abrams Books for Young Readers, 2007. Ever wonder what you should do if a deadly disaster hits? Read this book for tips on surviving terrorism, crime, hurricanes, tornadoes, floods, earthquakes, and more.

Steele, Philip. *Eyewitness City.* New York: DK Publishing, 2011. Learn more about the many kinds of cities across the globe in this fact-filled book.

Stewart, Melissa. *Inside Volcanoes.* New York: Sterling Children's Books, 2011. Wondering what makes scorching hot lava burst through Earth's crust? Read all about volcanoes in this book.

Verstraete, Larry. *At the Edge: Daring Acts in Desperate Times.* Toronto: Scholastic Canada, 2009. Read twenty-two real-life stories of kids, teens, and adults who faced life-threatening events and lived to tell the tales.

LERNER

Expand learning beyond the printed book. Download free, complementary educational resources for this book from our website, www.lerneresource.com.

SOURCE

PHOTO ACKNOWLEDGMENTS

The images in this book are used with the permission of: © Adam Jones/Visuals Unlimited, Inc., p. 4; © Jeff Rotman/Photodisc/Getty Images, p. 5; © Pacific Stock/ SuperStock, p. 6; © Michele Westmorland/The Image Bank/Getty Images, p. 7; © Julian Cohen/Flickr/Getty Images, p. 7 (inset); © Keystone/Hulton Archive/Getty Images, p. 8; © Mario Laporta/AFP/Getty Images, p. 9 (top); © iStockphoto.com/Floriano Rescigno, p. 9 (bottom); © AFP/Getty Images, pp. 10, 11; © iStockphoto.com/James Steidl, p. 11 (inset); © Richard Clark/Garden Picture Library/Getty Images, p. 12; © Jeff Greenberg/ Alamy, p. 13 (top); © E. Lessing/De Agostini/Getty Images, p. 13 (bottom); © Steve Winter/National Geographic/Getty Images, p. 14; © Animals Animals/SuperStock, p. 15; © Marcio Martins, p. 16; © NHPA/SuperStock, p. 17; © imagebroker.net/ SuperStock, p. 18; © Christopher Herwig/Lonely Planet Images/Getty Images, p. 19; © iStockphoto.com/Torsten Stahlberg, p. 19 (inset); © NaturePL/SuperStock, p. 20; © age fotostock/SuperStock, p. 21; © Imperial War Museums (SE 2256), p. 21 (inset); © Spencer Platt/Getty Images, p. 22; © Ville Palonen/Alamy, p. 23; © iStockphoto. com/Carlos Gawronski, p. 23 (inset); © Thierry Hennet/Flickr/Getty Images, p. 24; © Ariadne Van Zandbergen/Lonely Planet Images/Getty Images, p. 25 (top); © Richard Roscoe/Stocktrek Images/Getty Images, p. 25 (bottom); © Bernard Grua/Flickr/Getty Images, p. 26; © Bolot Bochkarev, p. 27 (both); © iStockphoto.com/Christian Wheatley, p. 28 (top); © Mary Evans Picture Library/Alamy, p. 28 (bottom); © Exactostock/ SuperStock, p. 29.

Front cover: © iStockphoto.com/Torsten Stahlberg.

Main body text set in Calvert MT Std Regular 11/16.
Typeface provided by Monotype Typography.